THIS *journal* BELONGS TO:

D1410925

Want free goodies?
Email us: gratitude@pbleu.com

@papeteriebleu

Papeterie Bleu

Shop our other books at
www.pbleu.com

Wholesale distribution through Ingram Content Group
www.ingramcontent.com/publishers/distribution/wholesale

For questions and customer service, email us at
support@pbleu.com

Develop an Attitude of Gratitude

"Make it a habit to tell people thank you. To express your appreciation, sincerely and without the expectation of anything in return. Truly appreciate those around you, and you'll soon find many others around you. Truly appreciate life, and you'll find that you have more of it."

~ Ralph Marston

`STEP #1:` Create a **HABIT**

- Start by setting the mood, in whatever way feels right for you. Here are a few suggestions that may get the grateful juices flowing...
  - Meditate
  - Pray
  - Have a hot cup of tea
  - Go for a walk
  - Light a fragrant candle
  - Find a quiet space
  - Unwind with a glass of vino
  - Listen to your favorite tune
  - Cuddle with your furry friend

- Reflect. This is your opportunity to think about it all... ALL OF IT! To appreciate gratefulness, you must also acknowledge hardships and struggles. Don't be afraid to explore your true thoughts and feelings about difficulties during the day. It is through adversity that we grow stronger. From the flames rises the phoenix. Consider the following questions...
  - What was hard for me? How did I react?
  - What did I overcome?
  - What am I thankful for?
  - How will I share my gratitude to enrich the lives of others?

- Put your thoughts to paper. The act of writing helps to consolidate your thoughts into memory- it's neuroscience! Sketch, draw, doodle, write, just go with YOUR flow!

`STEP #2:` **MAINTAIN** the practice

- Set a schedule.
  - Some studies show that it only takes 21 days to make a habit, while other studies cite up to nearly a year! Being grateful does not always come automatically. Those who set concrete goals are significantly more likely to stick with a new routine.
  - After each journaling session set a goal of the next time you plan to connect with yourself in this intimate setting.
  - Daily, weekly, after a hot yoga session... whatever feels RIGHT for YOU!

- Make time for yourself.
  Reserve a special time for you. You make time for what is important, and the practice of gratefulness is so enriching! Individuals who practice gratitude tend to...
  - Be more content with life
  - Have the ability to combat adversity with grace
  - Feel happier and more energetic
  - Sleep better
  - Have lower levels of stress hormones (translating to a stronger immune system!)
  - Be more likely to spread kindness and compassion to others

`STEP #3:` **SHARE** your light
  - Be kind to others
  - Be patient with their journey
  - Be grateful that you are grateful ☺

`THE LAYOUT EXPLAINED`

- **Inspiration**: Begin your gratitude session with a hand-picked thought on gratefulness to help guide your reflections.

- **Reflections**: Think about your day, your week, your year, your life! Nothing is too big or too small! How does an event make you feel? What would you do without the things in life you take for granted? How have you practiced gratefulness lately?

- **Grateful**: Relish in the gifts in life for which you are thankful!

- **Challenges**: Acknowledge things in life that have been difficult for you. Consider how those things have challenged you to grow stronger.

- **Goals**: How will you continue to incorporate gratitude into your life? How will you share it with others? When is the next time you want to dedicate time to yourself and developing a grateful spirit??

inspiration

It's not happiness that brings us gratitude. It's gratitude that brings us happiness.

Author Unknown

today

_____ / _____ / _____

reflections

grateful

challenges

goals

inspiration

Feeling gratitude and not expressing it is like wrapping a present and not giving it.

William Arthur Ward

today

/ /

reflections

grateful

challenges

goals

inspiration

Gratitude turns what we have into enough.

Melody Beattie

today

___/___/___

reflections

grateful

challenges

goals

inspiration

When you are grateful, fear disappears, and abundance appears.

Tony Robbins

today

/ /

reflections

grateful

challenges

goals

inspiration

Gratitude opens your eyes to the limitless potential of the universe, while dissatisfaction closes your eyes to it.
Stephen Richards

today

/ /

reflections

grateful

challenges

goals

inspiration

Gratitude is the healthiest of all human emotions. The more you express gratitude for what you have, the more likely you will have even more to express gratitude for. **Zig Ziglar**

today

/ /

reflections

grateful

challenges

goals

inspiration

Some people grumble that roses have thorns; I am grateful that thorns have roses.

Alphonse Karr

today

_/_/_

reflections

grateful

challenges

goals

inspiration

When you have an attitude of gratitude you wake up saying thank you.

Maya Angelou

today

/ /

reflections

grateful

challenges

goals

inspiration

Gratitude opens the door to the power, the wisdom, the creativity of the universe. You open the door through gratitude.
Deepak Chopra

today

/ /

reflections

grateful

challenges

goals

inspiration

Gratitude can transform common days into thanksgiving, turn routine jobs into joy, and change ordinary opportunities into blessings.
William Arthur Ward

today

/ /

reflections

grateful

challenges

goals

inspiration

Whatever you appreciate and give thanks for will increase in your life.

Sanaya Roman

today

/ /

reflections

grateful

challenges

goals

inspiration

The secret to having it all is knowing you already do.
Author Unknown

today

___/___/___

reflections

grateful

challenges

goals

inspiration

Gratitude is one of the most medicinal emotions we can feel, it elevates our moods and fills us with joy.

Sara Avant Stover

today

/ /

reflections

grateful

challenges

goals

inspiration

The real gift of gratitude is that the more grateful you are,
the more present you become.

Robert Holden

today

/ /

reflections

grateful

challenges

goals

inspiration

Showing gratitude is one of the simplest yet most powerful things humans can do for each other.

Randy Pausch

today

/ /

reflections

grateful

challenges

goals

inspiration

Be thankful for what you have; you'll end up having more.
If you concentrate on what you don't have, you will never,
ever have enough.   **Oprah Winfrey**

today

/ /

reflections

grateful

challenges

goals

inspiration

The miracle of gratitude is that it shifts your perception to such an extent that it changes the world you see.

Robert Holden

today

/ /

reflections

grateful

challenges

goals

inspiration

There is always, always, always something to be thankful for.
Author Unknown

today

/ /

reflections

grateful

challenges

goals

inspiration

A moment of gratitude makes a difference in your attitude.
Bruce Wilkinson

today

/ /

reflections

grateful

challenges

goals

inspiration

The struggle ends when gratitude begins.
Neale Donald Walsch

today

/ /

reflections

grateful

challenges

goals

inspiration

Gratitude unlocks all that's blocking us from really feeling truthful, really feeling authentic and vulnerable and happy.
Gabrielle Bernstein

today

/ /

reflections

grateful

challenges

goals

inspiration

Gratitude makes sense of your past, brings peace for today, and creates a vision for tomorrow.

Melody Beattie

today

/ /

reflections

grateful

challenges

goals

inspiration

In ordinary life, we hardly realize that we receive a great deal more than we give, and that it is only with gratitude that life becomes rich. **Deitrich Bonhoeffer**

today

___ / ___ / ___

reflections

grateful

challenges

goals

inspiration

The more grateful I am, the more beauty I see.

Mary Davis

today

/ /

reflections

grateful

challenges

goals

inspiration

Nothing new can come into your life unless you are grateful for what you already have.

Michael Bernhard

today

/ /

reflections

grateful

challenges

goals

inspiration

Through the eyes of gratitude, everything is a miracle.
Mary Davis

today

/ /

reflections

grateful

challenges

goals

inspiration

There is so much to be grateful for, just open your eyes.
Author Unknown

today

/ /

reflections

grateful

challenges

goals

inspiration

We often take for granted the very things that most deserve our gratitude.

Cynthia Ozick

today

/ /

reflections

grateful

challenges

goals

inspiration

Gratitude doesn't change the scenery. It merely washes clean the glass you look through, so you can clearly see the colors.
Richelle E. Goodrich

today

/ /

reflections

grateful

challenges

goals

inspiration

We can only be said to be alive in those moments when our hearts are conscious of our treasures.

Thornton Wilder

today

/ /

reflections

grateful

challenges

goals

inspiration

Sometimes we spend so much time and energy thinking about where we want to go that we don't notice where we happen to be.

Dan Gutman

today

/ /

reflections

grateful

challenges

goals

inspiration

The root of joy is gratefulness.

David Steindl-Rast

today

/ /

reflections

grateful

challenges

goals

inspiration

As we express our gratitude, we must never forget that the highest appreciation is not to utter words, but to live by them.

John F. Kennedy

today

___ / ___ / ___

reflections

grateful

challenges

goals

inspiration

Thankfulness creates gratitude which generates contentment that causes peace.

Tod Stocker

today

/ /

reflections

grateful

challenges

goals

inspiration

Happiness is a choice. You can choose to be happy. There's going to be stress in life, but it's your choice whether you let it affect you or not.
Valerie Bertinelli

today

/ /

reflections

grateful

challenges

goals

inspiration

Spread love everywhere you go. Let no one ever come
without leaving happier.

Mother Teresa

today

/ /

reflections

grateful

challenges

goals

inspiration

Happiness is not out there, it's in you.

Author Unknown

today

/ /

reflections

grateful

challenges

goals

inspiration

Give thanks for all of the opportunities that even our struggles bring.

Author Unknown

today

/ /

reflections

grateful

challenges

goals

inspiration

Gratitude dissolves negativity. Decide that no matter what comes your way, you'll find a grateful heart.

Author Unknown

today

/ /

reflections

grateful

challenges

goals

inspiration

Remember, being happy doesn't mean you have it all.
It simply means you're thankful for all you have.

Author Unknown

today

/ /

reflections

grateful

challenges

goals

inspiration

Do not take anything for granted- not one smile or one person or one rainbow or one breath, or one night in your cozy bed.
Terri Guillemets

today

/ /

reflections

grateful

challenges

goals

inspiration

Gratitude helps us to see what is there instead of what isn't.
Author Unknown

today

/ /

reflections

grateful

challenges

goals

inspiration

Be present in all things and thankful for all things.

Maya Angelou

today

/ /

reflections

grateful

challenges

goals

inspiration

When asked if my cup is half-full or half-empty, my only response is that I am thankful I have a cup.

Sam Lefkowitz

today

/ /

reflections

grateful

challenges

goals

inspiration

The roots of all goodness lie in the soil of appreciation for goodness.

Dalai Lama

today

/ /

reflections

grateful

challenges

goals

inspiration

When I started counting my blessings, my whole life turned around.

Willie Nelson

today

/ /

reflections

grateful

challenges

goals

inspiration

Reflect upon your present blessings, of which every man has plenty; not on your past misfortunes, of which all men have some.
Charles Dickens

today

/ /

reflections

grateful

challenges

goals

inspiration

Every single event in your life, especially the difficult lessons, have made you smarter, stronger, and wiser than you were yesterday. Be thankful!

Jenni Young

today

/ /

reflections

grateful

challenges

goals

inspiration

Gratitude helps you to grow and expand; gratitude brings joy and laughter into your life and into the lives of all those around you. **Eileen Caddy**

today

/ /

reflections

grateful

challenges

goals

inspiration

Gratitude drives happiness. Happiness boosts productivity. Productivity reveals mastery. And mastery inspires the world.

Robin S. Sharma

today

/ /

reflections

grateful

challenges

goals

inspiration

The more grateful I am, the more beauty I see.

Mary Davis

today

/ /

reflections

grateful

challenges

goals

inspiration

It is impossible to feel grateful and depressed in the same moment.

Naomi Williams

today

/ /

reflections

grateful

challenges

goals

inspiration

This is a wonderful day. I've never seen this one before.
Maya Angelou

today

/ /

reflections

grateful

challenges

goals

inspiration

Let us be grateful to the people who make us happy; they are the charming gardeners who make our souls blossom.

Marcel Proust

today

/ /

reflections

grateful

challenges

goals

inspiration

Count your rainbows, not your thunderstorms.

Alyssa Knight

today

/ /

reflections

grateful

challenges

goals

inspiration

Today I choose to live with gratitude for the love that fills my heart, the peace that rests within my spirit, and the voice of hope that says all things are possible. **Anonymous**

today

/ /

reflections

grateful

challenges

goals

inspiration

Gratitude is not only the greatest of virtues but the parent of all others.

Cicero

today

/ /

reflections

grateful

challenges

goals

inspiration

I was complaining that I had no shoes till I met a man who had no feet.

Confucius

today

/ /

reflections

grateful

challenges

goals

inspiration

Appreciation is a wonderful thing: It makes what is excellent in others belong to us as well.

Voltaire

today

/ /

reflections

grateful

challenges

goals

inspiration

An attitude of gratitude brings great things.

Yogi Bhajan

today

/ /

reflections

grateful

challenges

goals

inspiration

Gratitude and attitude are not challenges; they are choices.
Robert Braathe

today

/ /

reflections

grateful

challenges

goals

inspiration

Entitlement is such a cancer, because it is void of gratitude.
Adam Smith

today

/ /

reflections

grateful

challenges

goals

inspiration

"Enough" is a feast.

Buddhist proverb

today

/ /

reflections

grateful

challenges

goals

inspiration

Every blessing ignored becomes a curse.

Paulo Coelho

today

/ /

reflections

grateful

challenges

goals

inspiration

Things must be felt with the heart.

Helen Keller

today

/ /

reflections

grateful

challenges

goals

inspiration

The essence of all beautiful art is gratitude.

Friedrich Nietzche

today

/ /

reflections

grateful

challenges

goals

inspiration

Enjoy the little things, for one day you may look back and realize they were the big things.

Robert Brault

today

/ /

reflections

grateful

challenges

goals

inspiration

May the work of your hands be a sign of gratitude and reverence to the human condition.

Mahatma Gandhi

today

/ /

reflections

grateful

challenges

goals

inspiration

Three meals plus bedtime make four sure blessings a day.
Mason Cooley

today

/ /

reflections

grateful

challenges

goals

inspiration

When a person doesn't have gratitude, something is missing in his or her humanity.

Elie Wiesel

today

/ /

reflections

grateful

challenges

goals

inspiration

The best way to pay for a lovely moment is to enjoy it.
Richard Bach

today

/ /

reflections

grateful

challenges

goals

inspiration

Stop now. Enjoy the moment. It's now or never.

Maxime Lagacé

today

/ /

reflections

grateful

challenges

goals

inspiration

Wear gratitude like a cloak and it will feed every corner of your life.

Rumi

today

/ /

reflections

grateful

challenges

goals

inspiration

What separates privilege from entitlement is gratitude.
Brené Brown

today

/ /

reflections

grateful

challenges

goals

inspiration

Do not spoil what you have by desiring what you have not; remember that what you now have was once among the things you only hoped for.

Epicurus

today

/ /

reflections

grateful

challenges

goals

inspiration

There are only two ways to live your life. One is as though nothing is a miracle. The other is as though everything is a miracle.
Albert Einstein

today

/ /

reflections

grateful

challenges

goals

inspiration

When gratitude becomes an essential foundation in our lives, miracles start to appear everywhere.

Emmanuel Dalgher

today

/ /

reflections

grateful

challenges

goals

inspiration

He is a wise man who does not grieve for the things which he has not, but rejoices for those which he has.

Epictetus

today

/ /

reflections

grateful

challenges

goals

inspiration

When it comes to life, the critical thing is whether you take things for granted or take them with gratitude.

G.K. Chesterton

today

/ /

reflections

grateful

challenges

goals

inspiration

Gratitude is the sweetest thing in a seeker's life – in all human life. If there is gratitude in your heart, then there will be tremendous sweetness in your eyes. **Sri Chinmoy**

today

/ /

reflections

grateful

challenges

goals

inspiration

When we focus on our gratitude, the tide of disappointment goes out and the tide of love rushes in.

Kristin Armstrong

today

/ /

reflections

grateful

challenges

goals

inspiration

Happiness cannot be traveled to, owned, earned, worn, or consumed. Happiness is the spiritual experience of living every minute with love, grace, and gratitude. **Denis Waitley**

today

/ /

reflections

grateful

challenges

goals

inspiration

"Thank you" is the best prayer that anyone could say. I say that one a lot. "Thank you" expresses extreme gratitude, humility, understanding.
Alice Walker

today

/ /

reflections

grateful

challenges

goals

inspiration

So much has been given to me; I have no time to ponder over that which has been denied.

Helen Keller

today

/ /

reflections

grateful

challenges

goals

inspiration

As long as this exists, this sunshine and this cloudless sky, and as long as I can enjoy it, how can I be sad?

Anne Frank

today

/ /

reflections

grateful

challenges

goals

inspiration

True forgiveness is when you can say, "Thank you for that experience".

Oprah Winfrey

today

/ /

reflections

grateful

challenges

goals

inspiration

We must find time to stop and thank the people who make a difference in our lives.

John F. Kennedy

today

/ /

reflections

grateful

challenges

goals

inspiration

None is more impoverished than the one who has no gratitude. Gratitude is a currency that we can mint for ourselves, and spend without fear of bankruptcy.   **Fred De Witt Van Amburgh**

today

/ /

reflections

grateful

challenges

goals

inspiration

Develop an attitude of gratitude. Say thank you to everyone you meet for everything they do for you.

Brian Tracy

today

/ /

reflections

grateful

challenges

goals

inspiration

Be grateful for what you already have while you pursue your goals. If you aren't grateful for what you already have, what makes you think you would be happy with more. **Roy T. Bennett**

today

/ /

reflections

grateful

challenges

goals

inspiration

Silent gratitude isn't very much to anyone.

Gertrude Stein

today

/ /

reflections

grateful

challenges

goals

inspiration

Gratitude is riches. Complaint is poverty.

Doris Day

today

/ /

reflections

grateful

challenges

goals

inspiration

Gratitude is a quality similar to electricity: it must be produced and discharged and used up in order to exist at all.

William Faulkner

today

/ /

reflections

grateful

challenges

goals

inspiration

Gratitude is an opener of locked-up blessings.
Marianne Williamson

today

/ /

reflections

grateful

challenges

goals

inspiration

Gratitude is the ability to experience life as a gift. It liberates us from the prison of self-preoccupation.

John Ortberg

today

___ / ___ / ___

reflections

grateful

challenges

goals

inspiration

If you don't appreciate what you have, you may as well not have it.

Rosalene Glickman

today

/ /

reflections

grateful

challenges

goals

inspiration

Give thanks for a little and you will find a lot.

Hansa Proverb

today

/ /

reflections

grateful

challenges

goals

inspiration

What may seem a curse may be a blessing, and what may be a blessing may be a curse.

Muso Kokushi

today

/ /

reflections

grateful

challenges

goals

inspiration

The things you really need are few and easy to come by; but the things you can imagine you need are infinite, and you will never be satisfied.

Epicurus

today

/ /

reflections

grateful

challenges

goals

inspiration

Trade your expectations for appreciation and your whole world changes in an instant.

Tony Robbins

today

/ /

reflections

grateful

challenges

goals

Made in the USA
Monee, IL
10 March 2020